FAIRY CRAFTS

23 enchanting toys, gifts,
costumes and
party decorations

FAIRY CRAFTS

23 enchanting toys, gifts, costumes and party decorations

Heidi Boyd

NORTH LIGHT BOOKS
CINCINNATI, OHIO
www.artistsnetwork.com

Fairy Crafts: 23 enchanting toys, gifts, costumes and party decorations. Copyright © 2003 by Heidi Boyd. Printed in Singapore. All rights reserved. The patterns and drawings in the book are for the personal use of the reader. By permission of the author and publisher, they may be either hand-traced or photocopied to make single copies, but under no circumstances may they be resold or republished. It is permissible for the purchaser to make the projects contained herein and sell them at fairs, bazaars and craft shows. No other part of this book may be reproduced in any form or by any electronic or mechanical means including information storage and retrieval systems without permission in writing from the publisher, except by a reviewer, who may quote a brief passage in review. Published by North Light Books, an imprint of F&W Publications, Inc., 4700 East Galbraith Road, Cincinnati, Ohio 45236. (800) 289-0963. First edition.

Other fine North Light Books are available from your local bookstore or art supply store or direct from the publisher.

07 06 05 04 03   5 4 3 2 1
Library of Congress Cataloging-in-Publication Data
Boyd, Heidi.
Fairy crafts: 23 enchanting toys, gifts, costumes and party decorations / by Heidi Boyd.
      p.cm.
Includes index.
Summary: A brief story introduces different sections with detailed directions for making fairy toys, fairy costumes, and fairy gifts, as well as for preparing a fairy party.
ISBN 1-58180-430-X (pbk. : alk. paper)
1. Handicraft--Juvenile literature. 2. Fairies in art--Juvenile literature. 3. Fairies--Juvenile fiction. [1. Fairies in art. 2. Handicraft. 3. Costume. 4. Parties.] I. Title.

TT157.B72 2003
745.5--dc21
                          2003043044

Editors: Tricia Waddell and Jolie Lamping Roth
Designer: Stephanie Strang
Illustrations on pages 6, 12, 34, 52 and 70 by: Heidi Boyd
Production Coordinator: Michelle Ruberg
Layout Artist: Kathy Gardner
Photographers: Tim Grondin and Al Parrish
Photo Stylist: Jan Nickum

metric conversion chart

TO CONVERT	TO	MULTIPLY BY
Inches	Centimeters	2.54
Centimeters	Inches	0.4
Feet	Centimeters	30.5
Centimeters	Feet	0.03
Yards	Meters	0.9
Meters	Yards	1.1
Sq. Inches	Sq. Centimeters	6.45
Sq. Centimeters	Sq. Inches	0.16
Sq. Feet	Sq. Meters	0.09
Sq. Meters	Sq. Feet	10.8
Sq. Yards	Sq. Meters	0.8
Sq. Meters	Sq. Yards	1.2
Pounds	Kilograms	0.45
Kilograms	Pounds	2.2
Ounces	Grams	28.4
Grams	Ounces	0.04

ABOUT THE AUTHOR

Artist Heidi Boyd creates innovative craft projects for children using a philosophy toward surprise and accessibility. She's contributed proprietary projects to the kids' section of *Better Homes and Gardens*, *Crayola Kids* and *FamilyFun* magazines. Her work is featured in many Meredith Corporation's craft publications including *Crafts for Little Kids*, *Incredibly Awesome Crafts for Kids*, *Simply Handmade*, *Halloween Fun* and *501 Fun-to-Make Family Crafts*. With a degree in fine arts, she has been an art instructor to children in schools and art centers for over a decade while pursuing her vocation as an illustration artist. She lives in Des Moines, Iowa, with her husband, Jon, and sons, Jasper and Elliot.

DEDICATED
WITH LOVE
to Lewis and Karina Illingworth

Lily—adventurous and high-spirited, with an infectious laugh

Violet—shy and quiet, a very good friend to the small animals of the garden

Nana Rose—watches over all the fairies and flowers in the garden, is loved by all

Spot—Nana's jolly pet ladybug

Daisy—responsible and caring, but always ready for fun

Table of
CONTENTS

please come to a...

Flower Fairy Party
Saturday June 7th
from 2-4 pm
in the garden

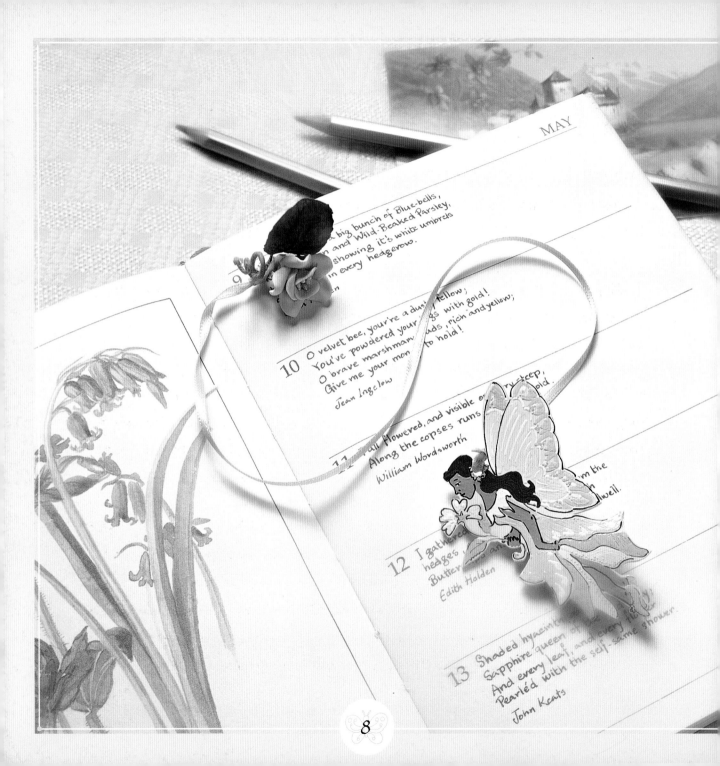

...big bunch of Blue-bells,
... and Wild Beaked Parsley,
... showing it's white umbrels
... in every hedgerow.

10 O velvet bee, you're a dusty fellow;
You've powdered your legs with gold!
O brave marshman... buds, rich and yellow;
Give me your mon... to hold!

Jean Ingelow

11 ...full flowered, and visible on every steep,
Along the copses runs ... old

William Wordsworth

...m the
...
...well.

12 I gathered...
hedges...
Butter... and...

Edith Holden

13 Shaded hyacinth...
Sapphire queen of...
And every leaf, and every flower
Pearléd with the self-same shower.

John Keats

INTRODUCTION

Imagine a hidden world of flower fairies in your very own garden.
Your children will embrace this fantasy when they follow the adventures of four charismatic fairies—
Lily, Daisy, Violet, Nana Rose—and their garden friends. The crafts that follow each story will
spur their creativity as they reenact the stories and create their own adventures while
making fairy dolls and dress-up clothes. They'll share their enthusiasm when they throw
their own fairy party and present handmade fairy-inspired gifts to friends and family.

Fun has been designed into every project. Your children will not only enjoy the process of making the crafts
but will delight in playing with the finished projects. Once they've learned the basic skills, they can easily add to
their toy collections by designing additional fairy dolls and play spaces. While making fairy crafts your children will,
I hope, discover the joy of creating their own toys. I vividly remember the puppets and stuffed animals I made
as a child. I'm confident that your children will take pride in and treasure their handmade fairy creations.

Easy-to-follow instructions will break the more complicated crafts into simple steps. The simplest of projects, such as
the Flower Sachets and Petal Bracelets, your children can make with the smallest amount of help. Other projects, like the
Fairyland Playground and Petal Skirts, will require you to take a more active role. Many other projects fall somewhere in
between. I hope you take the time to enjoy these projects with your children and learn together. I know firsthand that
children will treasure the time you take to craft with them. It's my sincere wish that this book will serve as a springboard
or your children's creativity and together you'll enjoy hours of sunshine and smiles in the land of flower fairies.

Heidi

getting started

The materials lists in this book feature standard arts and crafts supplies that should be readily available. A few specialized tools will make the projects easier, and some equipment requires adult supervision. Please take a moment to read the following before you start crafting with your child.

BASIC TOOLS

A small pair of **wire cutters** will come in handy to cut flower stems and floral wire. Thin stems and wire can often be cut with scissors, but they will nick the scissors blades. Attempting to cut heavy wire and floral stems with scissors is a dangerous undertaking both for children and adults. Wire cutters will make cutting easy and are worth the small investment to protect yourself and your scissors. They can be found in the jewelry section of craft stores or the tool section of hardware stores.

A small pair of **pliers** can also be found where wire cutters are sold and are helpful in shaping wire ends into spirals, and they are essential for squeezing crimp beads in the jewelry projects.

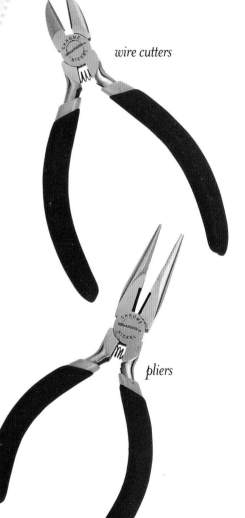

wire cutters

pliers

A **hot glue gun** is used in many of the craft projects. Please supervise your children when using a glue gun. I suggest a low-temperature smaller-size glue gun, which will be easier for older children to handle. The low setting will help prevent burns. Take the time to instruct them on the hazards of using this tool. I use a glue gun constantly when I'm crafting, but even after years of experience I will occasionally burn myself. I've found Beacon Kid's Choice glue to be a successful alternative to hot glue. It is thick enough to bond quickly (although still not as quick as hot glue) and often has stronger adhesion after it has dried. If you have any reservations about using a hot glue gun with your child, this product would be a good alternative. I have also specified specialized Beacon glues to use with craft foam (CraftFoam), floral foam (Hold the Foam), fabric (Fabri-Tac), and small beads (Gem-Tac). Sometimes other glues may initially bond these materials, but they'll pull apart after drying and will not withstand play. If you can't find Beacon glues, substitute craft or tacky glue.

hot glue gun

Using a **sewing machine** is an exciting skill for an older child to acquire with adult supervision. The Petal Purse in the Fairy Gifts chapter has two straight seams and is a great beginning machine-stitching project. Please be sure to sit with your child at the machine and discuss safety precautions, especially keeping fingers clear of the needle. The Petal Skirts in the Fairy Costumes chapter are more difficult because of the folded layers of cloth. Your child will learn a great deal from being your assistant in cutting and pinning the fabric and watching you machine stitch the skirts.

PLEASE NOTE: The projects in this book are intended for older children. Many contain small parts that are not suitable for children under three years of age.

Also, materials such as glitter spray and paint markers should be used in a well-ventilated area. Please supervise your children when using these materials.

sewing machine

A FAIRY ADVENTURE

"Whirlwind is on his way," Lily called from the top of the tallest hollyhock in the garden. Daisy and Violet braced themselves under the canopy of flowers for the rapid beating of the dragonfly's wings. "Where did you two go?" Lily wondered aloud as she peered over the edge of a crimson flower. Dewdrops rolled off the petals and splashed down onto Violet's and Daisy's wings. They both looked up to see Lily's flower tipping over the water's edge.

"Be careful!" warned Daisy. In an instant Whirlwind appeared and threw Lily one end of a vine. She quickly grabbed hold and flew down to the water, where Whirlwind treated her to a leaf ski around the pond. Daisy and Violet emerged from under the hollyhocks and shook out their wings. They chased each other down to the water's edge to join in the excitement.

"Whirlwind, may I have a ride, too?" shouted Daisy over the splashing water. Whirlwind quickly answered, "Most certainly!" Violet was so distracted watching her friends she didn't hear Flutter land quietly beside her. He tickled her cheek with his antennae to get her attention. "Oh, hello, Flutter," she said. He asked in reply, "Lovely day, isn't it?" Distracted by Daisy's and Lily's peals of laughter, she answered, "I guess . . . ." Trying to get her attention, Flutter asked, "Violet, did you know Robin laid two eggs in her nest in the magnolia tree?"

At this news Violet turned. "How exciting!" she exclaimed. "Would you like to see?" the butterfly asked. "Yes!" she replied, and in a second she was climbing onto Flutter's soft furry back. With a gentle swish of his wings they rose above the noise of the pond. Amidst the saucers of ivory petals she saw two beautiful blue eggs nestled in a sturdy twig nest.

fairy TOYS

RE-CREATE THE FAIRIES' MORNING AT THE POND,

OR IMAGINE YOUR OWN FAIRY ADVENTURES WITH

A HANDMADE SET OF FAIRY DOLLS AND

PLAYGROUND. DON'T STOP AFTER THESE

FIRST TWO PROJECTS IN THE TOY CHAP-

TER, AS YOU'LL ALSO WANT TO TREAT

YOUR FAIRIES TO A PEACEFUL NIGHT'S

SLEEP IN THE COMFORT OF THE FAIRY BASKET.

ONCE THE FAIRIES ARE TUCKED IN FOR THE NIGHT,

BECOME A FAIRY FASHION DESIGNER BY CREATING

A WARDROBE FOR THE DRESS-UP FAIRY DOLLS.

flower FAIRY DOLLS

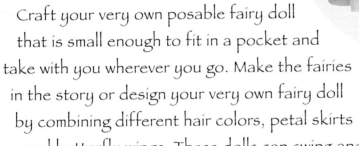

Craft your very own posable fairy doll
that is small enough to fit in a pocket and
take with you wherever you go. Make the fairies
in the story or design your very own fairy doll
by combining different hair colors, petal skirts
and butterfly wings. These dolls can swing and play in the Fairyland
Playground on page 20 and rest in the Fairy Basket on page 26.

WHAT YOU WILL NEED

- 16mm unfinished wood beads
- 22-gauge white cloth-wrapped wire (found in the floral department of craft stores)
- acrylic paint in assorted skin tones (I used Delta Ceramcoat Maple Sugar Tan 2062.)
- black acrylic paint (I used Delta Ceramcoat Black.)

- embroidery floss in a variety of different hair colors, such as brown, tan, red, yellow, white, silver and gold
- small to medium-size artificial flowers (Remove the plastic flower centers so you are left with fabric petal rings.)
- 16mm pearl beads
- ⅛" (3mm) wide ribbons (to tie in the finished fairy's hair)

- tiny flower bouquets (sold in the bridal department of craft stores)
- butterflies (The velvet variety are stronger than the feathered.)
- very small paintbrush (to paint facial features)
- wire cutters
- hot glue gun or Beacon Kid's Choice glue

1 To make a fairy other than the natural wood color, paint the wood bead and one floral wire the desired skin tone and let them dry completely. Use a small brush to paint the fairy's face. Make small dots for the eyes, a small dash for the nose and a wide smile. For added expression, paint arched eyebrows and carefully dot tiny eye-lashes around each eye. You can also use a fine-tipped marker, but it will work only on pre-painted beads, because the ink will bleed into the wood grain of an unfinished bead.

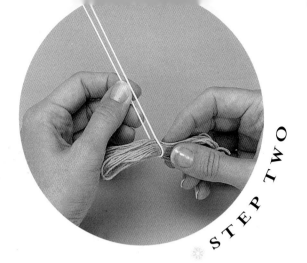

2 Cut the wire into two lengths, one 15" (38cm) long for the body and legs, and another 8" (20cm) long for the arms. To prepare the doll's hair, wind the embroidery floss (combine different shades of the same color of floss) around all four fingers of one hand to make a generous 4" (10cm) loop. Fold the 15" (38cm) wire in half and trap the center of the hair in the folded wire.

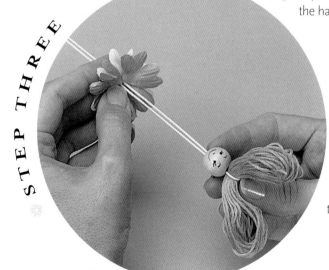

3 Thread the head bead through both ends of the wire and then slide it up as high as it will go under the hair. Next thread several small petal rings through both wires and slide them up to rest below the head.

4 To shape the arms, fold both ends of the 8" (20cm) wire in to the center. Squeeze the folded wires together to make two solid arms, leaving an open hand loop at either end.

5 Separate the two wires below the petals and slide the center of the arms between the wires. Join the wire ends back together and thread them both through a pearl bead. Slide the bead up the length of the wire, pushing it up under the center of the arms (it will help hold the arms in place).

6 Thread three or more larger petal rings through both wires. Slide the petals up under the pearl bead to make a generous flower skirt. To make the legs, separate the wires and fold each one in half, bringing the ends of the wires up under the petal skirt. Squeeze each set of the folded wires together as you did for the arms, leaving an open loop at the ends for a foot.

7 Cut the looped ends of the hair apart. There are many options for styling your fairy's hair. You can trim the ends shorter, braid it or tie it up with thin ribbons and glue a small flower to the crown of the head.

To make Nana Rose... *Combine silver and white embroidery floss for Nana Rose's hair. Do not cut the loop ends; instead, roll them up onto the top of her head in a loose bun and hot glue in place. Top the bun with a small red rose and leaves. Use layers of red rose petals to make a full skirt.*

8 Cut the antennae and wire end off the butterfly. Turn the fairy over and move the hair out of the way. Apply glue along the underside of the butterfly's body and glue it to the fairy's back. Now Daisy is ready to fly!

To make Lily... *First paint the wooden head bead and wires light brown. After the base coat has dried, paint the facial features onto the bead. Combine copper and brown embroidery floss to make Lily's hair. Separate the hair into three sections and then braid them together. Tie the ends with a small section of ribbon and then trim off the rounded loop ends below the ribbon. Glue a small pink flower onto her hair just above her forehead. Use pink lily flower petals for her skirt.*

To make Violet... *Combine bronze and light brown embroidery floss for Violet's hair. Cut the loop ends and let her hair hang loose. Hot glue small purple flowers and green leaves in a crown to the top of her head. Use purple morning glory petals topped with purple pansy petals to make her skirt.*

19

fairyland
PLAY
GROUND

This is the perfect place for your fairy dolls to play. They can swing on the vines, perch high in the flowers, play with Whirlwind and Hum (their dragonfly and hummingbird friends), dip in the water and have tea at the mushroom table and chairs. It will always be summer in your fairyland playground.

WHAT YOU WILL NEED

- 9" (23cm) round green floral foam disk, 1¼" (3.2cm) thickness
- two 8" x 10" (20cm x 25cm) green felt pieces
- 12" (30cm) round white floral foam disk, 1" (3cm) thickness
- 11" x 17" (28cm x 43cm) blue craft foam sheet
- 1 yard (1m) of iridescent fabric
- straight pins
- berry sprays

- bamboo skewers (available at grocery stores)
- purple anemone flowers
- 20" (51cm) lengths of ⅛" (3mm) diameter dowel rods
- 22- and 32-gauge green floral wire
- 3" (8cm) of 1½" (4cm) wide green ribbon
- tiny lavender and pink flower bouquets
- 2 blocks of pearl and 1 block of lavender polymer clay
- dragonfly

- feathered hummingbird
- 52" (1m) of ½" (1cm) wide off-white organza ribbon
- Beacon Hold the Foam glue or craft glue
- green floral tape
- scissors
- wire cutters
- hot glue gun

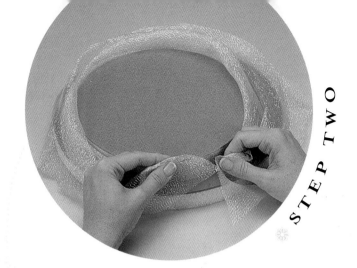

2   Cut a 2' x 2' x 3' (61cm x 61cm x 91cm) triangle of iridescent fabric. Working with the 3' (91cm) side of the fabric triangle, fold down the top 2" (5cm) and wrap the folded edge around the floral foam edge of the smaller disk. Glue and pin the fabric ends directly to the floral foam. Stretch the other edge of the fabric to cover the blue craft foam. '

1   Place the smaller disk over a sheet of felt and trace around the edges with a pencil. Remove the disk and follow your lines to cut out a felt circle. Apply foam or craft glue over the top surface of the small disk and then place the felt over the glue. Repeat the process with the larger disk and the blue craft foam. Glue the green disk over the blue disk, positioning it off to one side.

3   Fold the second piece of green felt lengthwise in thirds and cut along the fold lines. Cut the top edge of each of the three felt strips into uneven blades of grass. Glue the strips around the larger floral foam disk, covering the fabric edges. Use straight pins to hold the felt in place while the glue dries.

Use wire cutters to separate the berry spray into four pairs of berries, each with a leaf. Hold a pair of berries and leaf next to a bamboo skewer and wrap the two together with floral tape, working top to bottom. Repeat the process with the remaining three sets of berries.

Position two of the finished berry branches toward the back edge of the green disk. Push each of them through the felt (if necessary, first make a tiny slit with a scissors point), down into the floral foam and through to the craft foam cover of the first disk. Use scissors to carefully trim 4" (10cm) off the end of one of the remaining berry branches and then trim 2" (5cm) off the end of the other branch. Push these smaller branches through the felt on either side of the first two berry branches.

Use wire cutters to cut apart the anemone flower spray into three separate flowers with leaves. With scissors, carefully cut the dowel rod into 5" (13cm), 6" (15cm) and 9" (23cm) lengths. Hold a flower with leaves next to a dowel rod section and then wrap them together with floral tape, working top to bottom. Position the 9" (23cm) flowers between the first two berry branches and then press it down into the felt. Position the two remaining flowers on either side of the disk in front of the berry branches.

7 Using scissors, carefully cut a ⅛" (3mm) dowel rod into three bars 3"–5" (8cm–13cm). Verify the distance that these lengths will need to span between the berry branches and flower in your playground. Wrap each of the three bars in floral tape to completely conceal the wood. Span one of the bars between the center two berry branches. Wrap both sides of the bar to the berry branch with either a 3" (8cm) section of 32-gauge floral wire or the stem of one of the tiny lavender or pink flowers. Span the second bar between the first berry branch and the center flower. Span the third bar between the last two berry branches.

8 Cut two 9" (23cm) lengths of 32-gauge floral wire. Make a swing with a 3" (8cm) section of green ribbon. Fold under ¼" (6mm) of the cut edge of one side of the ribbon. Pinch the folded end in one hand and then wrap it three times with one end of the wires. Repeat the process with the other side of the ribbon swing.

9 Hang the swing from the center bar in the play space. Wrap each wire end three times around the bar.

23

10 Cut 7" (18cm) of 22-gauge floral wire and spiral one end of the wire around your fingertip. Wrap a small leaf from the tiny flower bouquet above the spiraled wire. Loop the other end of the finished swinging vine around the bar between the last two berry branches.

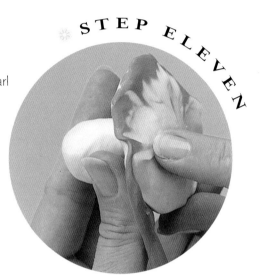

STEP ELEVEN

11 Mold a large mushroom with three-quarters of a brick of pearl polymer clay. Divide the remaining clay into three small mushrooms. Roll a generous pinch of lavender polymer clay into a long coil and wrap the coil around the edge of the mushroom caps. Use your thumb to blend the lavender clay up toward the center of the mushroom. To harden the finished mushrooms, bake the clay according to package directions.

STEP TWELVE

CAUTION

Supervise your children when using an oven.

12 Position the mushroom table and chairs under the flower toward the front edge of the felt-covered disk and glue in place. Push the iridescent fabric slightly aside and poke the dragonfly wire into the edge of the floral foam. Wrap the hummingbird wire around the base of the flower.

24

13 Hot glue tiny flowers and leaves randomly around the base of the playground. Encircle the bottom disk with off-white organza ribbon and tie the ribbon ends into a bow.

Use seasonal flowers to create additional playgrounds. Pastel-colored spring flowers combined with leftover Easter miniatures will excite any fairy with the promise of a new growing season. Use brightly colored silk fall leaves to make colorful blankets and hideaway tents in the branches of an autumn playland. For winter use holly and pine branches and make a frozen pond out of foil and artificial snow for a fairy skating rink.

fairy BASKET

Every night tuck your fairy dolls into the hammock, where they'll sleep to the music of crickets and wake to Bumble's buzzing and the singing of birds. The fairy basket is the perfect place to keep your fairy dolls. It makes a beautiful addition to your room and is portable so you can take it to your friend's house to play.

WHAT YOU WILL NEED

- pussy willow branch
- small purple climbing rose
- small basket with handle (I used an 8" [20cm] wide round basket, 10" [25cm] tall with handle.)
- off-white daisies
- small yellow flowers with grasslike leaves

- bumblebee
- cricket
- feathered butterfly
- pair of small feathered birds (I used a male and female nuthatch.)
- small bird's nest
- ½ yard (46cm) of 1½" (4cm) wide green ribbon

- pair of small speckled plastic bird eggs
- 1 yard (1m) of 1½" (4cm) wide purple ribbon
- 1 yard (1m) of light green tulle
- wire cutters
- hot glue gun

1 Use wire cutters to separate individual pussy willow branches and rose stems. Wind the individual stems around the basket handle. Make sure the top of a pussy willow branch extends a couple of inches out from the top of the handle, because you will need it later to hang the hammock. Anchor the bottom ends of the stems and branches by threading them into the basket weave. If necessary, use hot glue to hold them in place.

2 Clip individual rose and daisy flowers off their stems and hot glue the flowers around the base of both sides of the basket handle.

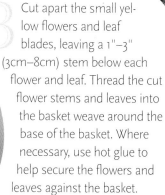

3 Cut apart the small yellow flowers and leaf blades, leaving a 1"–3" (3cm–8cm) stem below each flower and leaf. Thread the cut flower stems and leaves into the basket weave around the base of the basket. Where necessary, use hot glue to help secure the flowers and leaves against the basket.

4   Cut away any wires that might be attached to the bumblebee, cricket and butterfly. Hot glue the bumblebee's feet to the center of a purple rose along the rim of the basket. Hot glue the underside of the cricket's body and his feet to the side of the basket between the yellow flowers and leaf blades. Finally, hot glue the underside of the feathered butterfly's body to the rim of the basket between the daisy flowers.

STEP FOUR

5   Wrap the wire that extends from the female bird's feet around the top edge of the bird's nest. Place the green ribbon inside the nest and then place the speckled bird eggs into the ribbon-lined nest. Position the nest to one side of the basket at the base of the basket handle. If you're using a twiggy nest, you'll be able to get the nest to stay in place by pushing some of the twigs into the inner basket weave; if not, apply a generous amount of hot glue to anchor the nest in place.

STEP FIVE

6   Fold 2' (61cm) of purple ribbon in half and then loop the fold over the top pussy willow branch. Bring one ribbon end over the top of the basket handle and the other end down through the handle. Join the ends back together, hot gluing one end over the other. Hot glue the joined ribbon to the top of the basket handle.

STEP SIX

Wrap the wire that extends below the male bird's feet around the basket handle. Tie a bow with the remaining purple ribbon and trim off any extra ribbon. Glue the underside of the bow to the handle to conceal both the bird wire and hammock connections. Line the basket with tulle to soften your fairy storage space.

Silk flower reproductions are made for almost all of the flowers found in the garden. Experiment with different flower combinations. The key is to use tiny, small and medium-size flowers in conjunction with a branched flower such as pussy willow, forsythia or dogwood.

Dress~up FAIRY DOLLS

This toy inspires creativity from start to finish! You design the hairstyle, wings, clothing and accessories when you first assemble the doll, and then each time you play, you can combine the pieces in different ways. The hook-and-loop fastening system is easy for a young child to manipulate.

WHAT YOU WILL NEED

- 8" x 10½" (20cm x 27cm) three-ring binder photo album
- craft foam sheets in a variety of skin tones, colors and patterns
- ½" (1cm) wide hook-and-loop fasteners
- precut craft foam pieces in flower, butterfly and dragonfly shapes

- assorted rhinestones
- zippered and prepunched plastic sleeve (sold with school supplies to hold pens and pencils)
- Beacon CraftFoam glue (Other glues may not withstand the pulling and pushing of dressing and undressing the doll.)

- pencil
- scissors
- paper punch
- permanent fine-tipped black marker
- ballpoint pen
- patterns (pages 86–87)

1 Remove the photo sleeves from the album and set one aside to be a pattern for your fairy doll page. Lay the photo sleeve over a craft foam sheet. Use a pencil to trace around all four sides and inside the punched holes of the photo sleeve. Remove the photo sleeve, cut along the pencil lines and punch through the traced circles with a paper punch. Use the patterns provided to cut the doll's body, head and hair out of skin tone and solid colored craft foam sheets. With the permanent marker, draw the fairy's face onto the bottom two-thirds of the head. Apply glue to the underside of all the pieces and then place them in the center of the prepared foam page.

2 Use just the hook portion of the hook-and-loop fasteners to attach to the fairy doll and foam page. The loop portion will be used later and glued to the back of the clothing, wings and accessory pieces. Cut a 1½" (4cm) strip and then glue it down the center of the fairy's body. Cut a 1" (3cm) strip and glue it across the fairy's abdomen. Cut two more 2" (5cm) strips and then cut a small arch into the end of each piece so they'll fit over the fairy's shoulders. Position them at an angle extending above each shoulder and glue them directly to the foam page. Cut and glue a ¾" (1cm) half circle over the hair. Using a paper punch, punch a small circle from the hook fastener (or cut a small circle with scissors) and glue it to one of the fairy's hands. The glue will need to dry overnight. If necessary, use a heavy book to weight the hook fastener against the foam while it dries.

4 Cut 1"–1½" (3cm–4cm) strips of the loop portion of the hook-and-loop fasteners. Glue the loop strips to the back of the foam pieces, lengthwise down the wings, vertically down the center of the shirts and across the top of the skirts and pants. Allow the glued strips to dry overnight.

3 Trace the clothing, wings and accessory patterns onto patterned and solid colored craft foam sheets (use pencil on the light-colored foam; ballpoint pen works better on the dark-colored foam). Continue tracing and cutting out clothing in a variety of different colored and patterned foam. The more choices you have to play with, the more fun your dress-up fairy will be.

5 Decorate the cutout clothing pieces by gluing on precut flowers and rhinestones, and then let the glue dry completely.

6 Use the precut butterfly and dragonfly shapes as a base to make pets for your fairy to hold in her hand. Cut antennae and a body shape out of craft foam scraps and glue them along with a small rhinestone head onto the butterfly and dragonfly. Glue a small dot of loop fastener to the underside of the finished butterfly and dragonfly. Store the finished accessories, clothes and wings in the zippered case. Clip both the foam page and case into the binder for easy storage.

STEP SIX

Take advantage of the wide variety of patterned craft foams and rhinestones to make interesting clothes and accessories. The more pieces you make, the more interesting the finished toy will be, providing endless fashion combinations.

33

A SPECIAL INVITATION

The sun was streaming through the rose petals above the fairies' hammock. Violet stirred at the sound of Bumble's approach. As the bee passed overhead, Violet waved. He loosened a letter from his sack and dropped it at her feet. Careful not to wake her friends, she opened the letter. "Ohhh!" she squealed in excitement. "What's happening?" asked Daisy as she wiped the sleep from her eyes. "We're invited to a party tonight at Nana Rose's!" Violet carefully whispered this time. "Oh, there's nothing that's more fun than a party at Nana's!" she exclaimed as she made a sudden leap out of the hammock. The hammock rocked wildly and stirred Lily out of a deep sleep. "How can a fairy get any rest in this garden?" she grumped with her eyes still closed.

"Have you heard the news?" asked Hum, the hummingbird, as he zoomed over from the honeysuckle. "Yes!" shouted Violet and Daisy. This time with her eyes wide open Lily demanded, "What is all the commotion about?" In unison, Hum, Violet and Daisy explained, "There's a party tonight at Nana Rose's." Lily cried, "Yippee!" as she flipped through the air and landed with such force on the leaf swing that she slipped off and fell into a mud puddle. "Oh, dear," she remarked as she lifted the sides of her mud-soaked petal skirt. "I guess we could all use a fresh set of petals for the party," decided Daisy.

Lucky for the fairies the warm sun had unfurled a beautiful array of new flowers in the garden. After breakfast the fairies picked up their petal purses and flower wands and went their separate ways in the garden. Lily found beautiful lily flowers with petals spotted in lilac and edged in pink. She took a single petal from each flower and gently folded them into her purse. Before leaving, she tapped each flower with her wand and new petals magically replaced the ones she had picked. Back at the pond's edge, she found Violet and Daisy comfortably installed on mushroom seats, stitching their petals with glistening strands of a spiderweb.

fairy COSTUMES

EVERY FAIRY NEEDS A TOUCH OF MAGIC,

WHICH IN THE COSTUME CHAPTER COMES

IN THE FORM OF A SPARKLING BERIBBONED

FLOWER WAND. LET YOUR IMAGINATION

TAKE FLIGHT WHEN YOU WEAR A

MATCHING SHIMMERING SET OF FAIRY

WINGS. TO MATCH YOUR PARTY OUTFIT TO

ROSE'S, DAISY'S OR VIOLET'S, FASHION A

COORDINATING HALO, HEADBAND OR

CHOKER AND ADD FLOWERS TO YOUR SHOES.

fairy WAND

Pick your favorite flower to place on the
end of your wand. When you wave your finished
wand in the air, the ribbons flutter and the
beaded fringe swings. Bring your wand into
the garden to cast growing spells
on the flowers and trees.

WHAT YOU WILL NEED

- 2' (61cm) each of ¼" (6mm) wide green, light and dark pink, lavender and iridescent ribbon
- 18" (46cm) length of ¼" (6mm) diameter dowel rod
- 6" (15cm) of ⅜" (1cm) wide ribbon with beaded fringe
- large silk flower that has a fabric leaf section directly under the flower

- 2' (61cm) of 1½" (4cm) wide sheer green ribbon
- 32-gauge floral wire
- plastic berry bead (or plastic pearl bead)
- hot glue gun
- wire cutters

38

1 Hot glue the end of the ¼" (6mm) wide green ribbon to the top of the dowel rod. Spiral the ribbon down the length of the dowel rod and anchor every other wrap in place with a small dot of glue. Starting 3"–4" (8cm–10cm) down from the top of the dowel rod, hot glue the ribbon end of the beaded fringe to the rod and wrap it up toward the top of the rod. Add a drop of hot glue under each wrap to hold the fringe in place. Make sure the beads do not get trapped under the ribbon, so they swing freely when the wand is waved.

STEP ONE

2 Use wire cutters to remove the flower from the stem. Pull off the leaves under the flower and thread them onto the end of the dowel. Apply a generous amount of glue to the underside of the flower and glue it over the top of the dowel rod. Glue the tops of the threaded leaves to the underside of the rose.

STEP TWO

STEP THREE

3 Group the 2' (61cm) lengths of ¼" (6mm) wide ribbon together, and in one motion tie the center of the grouped ribbons around the dowel rod just under the rose. Tie the wide sheer green ribbon over the tied ¼" (6mm) wide ribbons and then tie the wide sheer green ribbon ends into a bow.

4 Thread 4" (10cm) of floral wire through the berry bead. Apply glue to one side of the bead and place it glue side down over the end of the dowel rod. Wrap the wire ends around the end of the dowel rod and trim the ends.

STEP FOUR

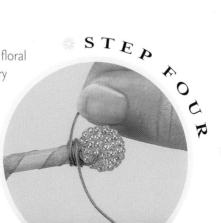

petal SKIRTS

The same steps are used to make the rose, daisy and violet skirts. Only the patterns, fabric colors and silk flowers change to make the different styles. Wear the finished petal skirt over tights and a leotard. It's hard to keep still when wearing a petal skirt that begs to be twirled.

WHAT YOU WILL NEED

FOR ALL THE SKIRTS, YOU WILL NEED:

- ½ yard (46cm) white sequined elastic (Wrap the elastic around your child's waist to determine the exact length, and add an extra 1" [3cm] for a joining seam.)
- scissors
- straight pins
- sewing machine and white thread
- hot glue gun or Fabri-Tac glue
- skirt pattern (pages 88-89)

TO MAKE EACH INDIVIDUAL SKIRT, ADD THE FOLLOWING FABRIC AND FLOWERS:

Rose Petal Skirt *(above)*

- 1¼ yards (1.1m) of 44" (112cm) wide pink pearlescent sheer fabric
- 2½ yards (2.3m) of 54" (137cm) wide pink shiny tulle fabric
- approximately eight rose silk flowers (stems removed)

Violet Petal Skirt *(page 43)*

- 1 yard (1m) of 44" (112cm) wide violet pearlescent sheer fabric
- 1½ yards (1.4m) of 54" (137cm) wide light purple shiny tulle fabric

- ½ yard (.5m) of 42" (107cm) wide Mermaid Pearls abalone purple fabric
- approximately seven pansy silk flowers (stems removed)

Daisy Petal Skirt *(page 43)*

- ¾ yard (69cm) of 42" (107cm) wide Mermaid Pearls white fabric
- 1¼ yards (1.1m) of 44" (112cm) wide white pearlescent sheer fabric
- 1¼ yards (1.1m) of 54" (137cm) wide white shiny tulle fabric
- approximately seven daisy silk flowers (stems removed)

NOTE: If you cannot find Mermaid Pearls fabric, use a heavyweight opaque iridescent fabric.

40

1 FOR THE ROSE PETAL SKIRT: Use the rose petal pattern to cut out four pink pearlescent sheer petals and cut eight pink shiny tulle petals. Stack two shiny tulle petals over each of the pearlescent petals.

FOR THE DAISY PETAL SKIRT: Cut seven large petals out of the Mermaid Pearls white fabric and cut fourteen white pearlescent sheer and twenty-one white shiny tulle of the smaller petal pattern. Spread the seven large petals out on the table and stack a group of three white tulle and two white pearlescent over each large petal.

FOR THE VIOLET PETAL SKIRT: Cut four large petals out of the violet pearlescent sheer fabric, twelve medium petals out of the light purple shiny tulle and four small petals out of the Mermaid Pearls abalone purple. Lay the four pearlescent petals out on the table and stack three tulle petals and one Mermaid Pearls abalone purple petal over each large petal.

2 FOR THE ROSE PETAL SKIRT: Make two folds along the top edge of a pair of tulle petals. Hold the folded edge against the top of the pearlescent petal and pin all three layers to the edge of the precut sequin waistband.

FOR THE DAISY AND VIOLET PETAL SKIRTS: Make the same folds along the top edge of the white pearlescent and purple Mermaid Pearls petals (the smallest petals at the top of each stack). Pin them along with the petals under each grouping to the waistband.

3 Repeat the folding and pinning process with the remaining sets of petals. Space the petal groups evenly along the waistband. If you're making a skirt for a larger child, you may want to add an additional grouping of petals, and conversely for a smaller child, you may choose to eliminate a set of petals.

41

Machine stitch the pinned petals to the elastic in four separate sections of stitching. (If you sew continuously through the waistband, you'll prevent it from freely expanding and contracting.) Reinforce the beginning and end of each section by backstitching for 1" (3cm).

Working on the wrong side of the skirt, bring the elastic ends together. Machine stitch the width of the elastic several times for a secure connection.

Turn the skirt right side out. Apply hot glue or Fabri-Tac to the underside of one silk flower at a time and hot glue them to the waistband, centered over each set of fabric petals. Hot glue more flowers centered between the first four.

She loves me, she loves me not. . . . There's no question that any flower fairy will love this costume. A flurry of white petals not only make Daisy's skirt, but crown her head, decorate her wings and touch the toes of her shoes.

After finishing Violet's swirling skirt, add a touch of purple to a pair of wings with several more pansy flowers. Save the remaining small pansy flowers and leaves to make a charming choker and to add a final splash of purple to her shoes.

fairy WINGS

Lighten your step and slip on a pair of fairy wings. These wings are simple to make and sturdy enough to last through many fairy dress-up adventures. To make wings to match the daisy and violet costumes, simply switch the flowers to match your petal skirt.

WHAT YOU WILL NEED

- two white wire hangers
- children's white tights size 7–10 (48"–55" [122cm–140cm] in 55–72 lbs. [25kg–33kg])
- three silk flowers (roses, daisies or pansies)
- silver glitter spray
- 30" (76cm) of ¼" (6mm) wide elastic
- duct tape
- hot glue gun
- safety pin
- needle and thread

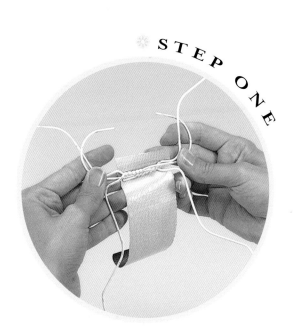

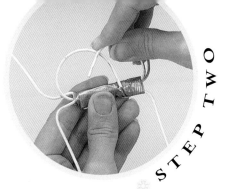

Bend the rounded hanger ends down over the tape. This will help prevent the tights from snagging on the wire ends.

Position the hangers together end to end. Wrap 4" (10cm) of duct tape around the flat twisted wire below the hooks.

Push out the bends in both hangers and shape each hanger into a butterfly wing.

Thread the waist of the tights down over the top of the wire wing frame. Continue sliding the tights down over the frame. Each leg will cover a wing.

Pull the waist of the tights up and around the taped connection between the wings. Wrap it several times and hot glue the bunched waistband over the wrapped tights.

Hot glue three silk flowers over the glued tights. Tuck a couple of leaves on either side of the flowers and hot glue them to the tights under the flowers.

STEP SIX

Move to a well-ventilated area. Working over a protected surface, spray the edges of the wings silver. For added drama, lightly spray the edges of the flowers.

STEP SEVEN

STEP EIGHT

Center the ¼" (6mm) elastic over the underside of the wings and bring both ends to the center to form two loops. Safety pin the ends to the center of the elastic and have your child place her arms through the loops to test the fit across the back of her shoulders. If the elastic sags down your child's back, you'll need to trim either end of the elastic to shorten the loops. Once the elastic length has been adjusted, stitch through all three layers into the tights on the underside of the wings.

46

fairy SHOES

Transform any plain shoe into fairy footwear with the addition of small silk flowers and leaves. Nothing makes the fairy transformation more complete than to be dressed up from head to toe.

WHAT YOU WILL NEED

❀ white shoes
❀ small silk flowers and leaves (roses, daisies or pansies)
❀ wire cutters
❀ hot glue gun

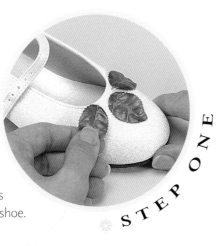

STEP ONE

1 Cut six small leaves and flowers off the flower stems. Hot glue three leaves over the toe of each shoe.

STEP TWO

2 Apply hot glue to the underside of each flower and glue them over the tops of the leaves. Place the larger flowers in the center and the smaller flowers on either side.

Rose HALO

Every child is an angel at heart and should be crowned in a halo of flower petals. This halo can be made in other colors with different silk flowers to match any of the skirt-and-wing ensembles.

WHAT YOU WILL NEED

- 2' (61cm) of petal roping (or 22-gauge floral wire)
- small trailing rose bush
- four to five large roses in the same color
- wire cutters
- hot glue gun

STEP ONE

Form a 2' (61cm) length of wired petals into a circle. Twist the ends together to hold the halo shape.

STEP TWO

Cut 3" (8cm) rose stems off the bush and wrap them around the halo. The wire will help hold the rose stems in place.

Cut four to five larger roses off their stems and hot glue them around the front of the halo to fill any bare spots.

STEP THREE

Daisy HEAD BAND

Transform a headband into a fairy crown of ribbons and flowers. For everyday wear, make the headband without the trailing ribbons.

WHAT YOU WILL NEED

- ✿ child-size plain headband (fabric-covered works best)
- ✿ 2' (61cm) of 1½" (4cm) wide white spotted wire-edged ribbon
- ✿ silk flowers (stems removed)
- ✿ two sets of 3' (91cm) of ¾" (2cm) wide sheer ribbon in green, white and yellow
- ✿ 4" (10cm) sections of white or green 32-gauge floral wire
- ✿ hot glue gun

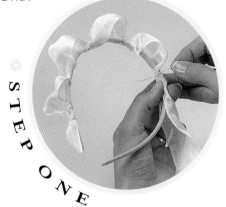

STEP ONE

1 Starting at one end of the headband, tuck the edge of the white spotted ribbon under the headband and secure it with a length of wire to hold it in place. Work your way around the headband, repeating the wrapping process every 1½"–2" (4cm–5cm).

STEP TWO

2 After removing the leaves, apply hot glue to the underside of the flowers and press them over a section of wrapped wire and ribbon. Glue flowers until all the wrapped wire sections are covered.

STEP THREE

3 Tie the center of one set of ribbons around each end of the headband. Skip this last step and use small flowers if you're making the headband for everyday wear.

49

Violet CHOKER

Save small silk flowers and combine them with pearls
and sheer ribbon to make a beautiful choker. This choker
can be made with thinner ribbon to become everyday
jewelry that accompanies a simple shirt or dress.

WHAT YOU WILL NEED

- small silk pansies
- 2' (61cm) of 1½" (4cm) sheer purple ribbon
- small pearl beads
- plastic pony bead

- four leaves
- wire cutters
- hot glue gun or Gem-Tac glue

1 Use wire cutters to cut the flowers off the flower stems. Pull the plastic centers out from each of the flowers and stack each set of flower petals together. Lay the ribbon flat on a protected work surface (use old plastic place mats or a vinyl tablecloth; paper will stick to the underside of the choker). Apply a small amount of hot glue or Gem-Tac to the underside of one set of petals and glue them to the center of the ribbon. Apply a small dot of hot glue to the center of a pearl bead and glue it to the center of the flower. Continue gluing pansies 1"–1½" (3cm–4cm) apart down the length of the ribbon, leaving 3"–4" (8cm–10cm) of plain ribbon on either end. If you enjoy sewing, stitch the petals and beads to the ribbon to secure.

2 Bring the ribbon ends together and thread them both through the pony bead.

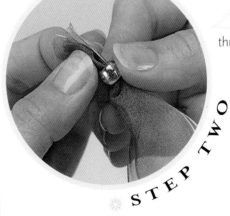

3 Cut four leaves off the discarded flower stems. Hot glue a pair of leaves to each ribbon end, trapping the ribbon between the layers. Hot glue a flower with a pearl center over the top two leaves.

NANA'S PARTY

The fairies chatted in excitement while stitching their new petal skirts. "I collected some tiny violets to sugar for Nana Rose," shared Violet. "Oh, that's a great idea," agreed Daisy. "That reminds me . . . Nana loves raspberry nectar, too. Lily, when we're finished, could you help me collect the nectar?" A smiling Lily replied, "I'd love to. You know I love to climb to the top of the brambles." Daisy chided, "Not in your new skirt. It'll be torn to shreds on the thorns." Lily said, "Of course not. We should wait until nightfall to change into our new petals."

The rest of the day passed quickly as the fairies made preparations for the party. Lily and Rose collected sweet raspberry nectar, and Violet busied herself sugaring the tiny flowers by dipping them in Bumble's sweet honey. The sky above the climbing rose became streaked with pinks and purples, and the cricket songs started to fill the air. The fairies splashed their hands and faces in cool lavender water. With three quick twirls, they were instantly dressed in their new petal skirts. They reached for their flower wands and raised them over their heads. A stream of sparkling fairy dust spiraled around them and shimmered over their hair, wings and new skirts. With beribboned packages in hand, they skipped merrily down the garden path. "Watch out, Lily, you'll spill the nectar," cautioned Daisy. "Don't worry, Daisy, I . . . ," Lily paused.

At that moment their eyes were drawn to the clearing under the tea rose bush and they stopped in their tracks. In the evening's dusk Nana's nook was glittering with the most beautiful pinks, purples and yellows found in the garden. Fireflies illuminated every flower lantern hanging over the tables and dance floor. "Welcome, girls," beckoned Nana. The fairies joined hands and rushed to the party. Everyone had a wonderful evening sharing delicious food, laughter, songs and dances.

fairy PARTY

SET THE SCENE FOR A TRULY MAGICAL FAIRY PARTY.

HAVE YOUR ROOM LIT WITH FAIRY LANTERNS,

AND SET THE TABLE WITH BLOOMING

PLATES, FLOWER FLUTES TOPPED WITH

SHIMMERING BUTTERFLY STRAWS, AND

TABLEWARE SETS WITH SWEET LOLLIPOP

BUMBLE BEES NESTLED IN THE FOLDS OF

THE NAPKIN LEAVES. THE PETAL BRACELET

PARTY ACTIVITY WILL KEEP GUESTS CREATIVELY

ENTERTAINED WHILE MAKING A LASTING

MEMENTO OF A SPECIAL AFTERNOON.

Firefly LANTERNS

Dress up a string of purchased paper lanterns or a single lantern to make these festive floral lights. The finished lights can be used year-round to brighten a child's room and bring the summer indoors on a dark winter's day.

WHAT YOU WILL NEED

- 8½" x 11" (22cm x 28cm) sheets of tissue paper, assorted colors (If making a single big lantern, you'll need large sheets, such as the sheets packaged for wrapping tissue.)

- string of paper lanterns or a large single lantern (sold in craft and import stores)
- 5¼" (13cm) of ⅜" (1cm) wide ribbon with beaded trim (for each lantern)
- pencil

- scissors
- hot glue gun
- glue stick
- flower pattern (page 91)

Fold an 8½" x 11" (22cm x 28cm) sheet of tissue paper in half and then in half again. Fold the remaining quarter in half again to make a triangle. Line up the pattern against the folded side of the triangle. (The pattern won't reach the folded point.) Use a pencil to trace the top and bottom edges of the pattern onto one side of the folded tissue. To make a large single lantern, fold a large sheet of tissue paper the same way and draw the same petals, only larger to fill the triangle. Adjust the center circle opening to fit your lantern.

STEP ONE

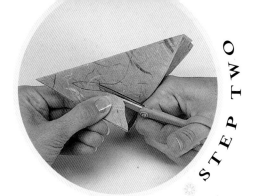

Remove the pattern and use scissors to cut along the pencil lines. Be sure to cut through all the folded layers of tissue paper. Carefully unfold the cut paper shape into a flower with a hole in the center. Repeat the process with a different-colored sheet of tissue paper to make a second flower.

Slide a single lantern off the string of lights or assemble the lantern if purchased flat. Hot glue the ribbon edge of the beaded trim around the bottom circle opening of the lantern. The beads should hang down freely.

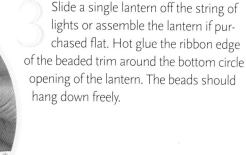

STEP THREE

STEP FOUR

Apply the glue stick around the rim of one of the tissue paper flowers and position it over the top opening of the lantern. Repeat the process with the second flower and glue it over the first. Repeat steps 1-4 for each remaining lantern and restring.

fairy INVITATIONS

Layers of vellum and paper combine to make a pretty flower card that opens to reveal a tiny fairy flying through the flower's center. This engaging card will foster excitement for your upcoming party. Or just make a single card to send a little magic to a friend who's feeling blue.

Please come to a....

Flower Fairy Party
Saturday June 7th
from 2-4 pm
in the garden

WHAT YOU WILL NEED

- blue, pink, purple and green cardstock
- blue, pink, purple and green vellum sheets
- skin-tone paper
- small silk flower petals (stems and flower centers removed)
- doll hair (or yarn or embroidery floss)

- 3¾" x 6½" (10cm x 17cm) white vellum envelopes (for mailing)
- Beacon Kid's Choice glue or craft glue
- glue stick
- pencil
- scissors
- fine-tipped black marker

- small (approximately ¾" [2cm]) silk flower bouquet (sold in the bridal craft section in craft stores)
- gold or silver paint markers
- patterns (page 90)

58

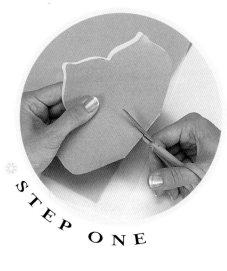

Fold a sheet of blue, pink or purple cardstock in half and line up the pattern against the folded edge. Trace the petal pattern with a pencil. Cut through both layers of paper to cut out the petal-shaped card. Repeat the process with a matching sheet of vellum and then slip the vellum card inside the paper card. Line up the two card layers and make two center slits through the folded edge.

STEP TWO

Place the fairy pattern over a sheet of skin-tone paper. Trace the pattern with a pencil. Cut the fairy out and use a fine-tipped black marker to give her small dots for eyes and an upturned dash for a mouth. Use Beacon Kid's Choice glue to glue small petals over her body to make a dress. Glue a small amount of doll hair to the top of her head. Glue her hand folded down over a small flower stem. (Don't get carried away decorating this fairy. The key is to make sure she's lightweight so she fits inside the petal card.)

STEP THREE

Open the card and slide your forefinger behind the card and push the paper strip between the slits into the center of the card. Glue the back of the fairy's knee to the front of the popped-out paper strip. Open and close the card to test that the fairy fits properly so adjustments can be made before the glue dries.

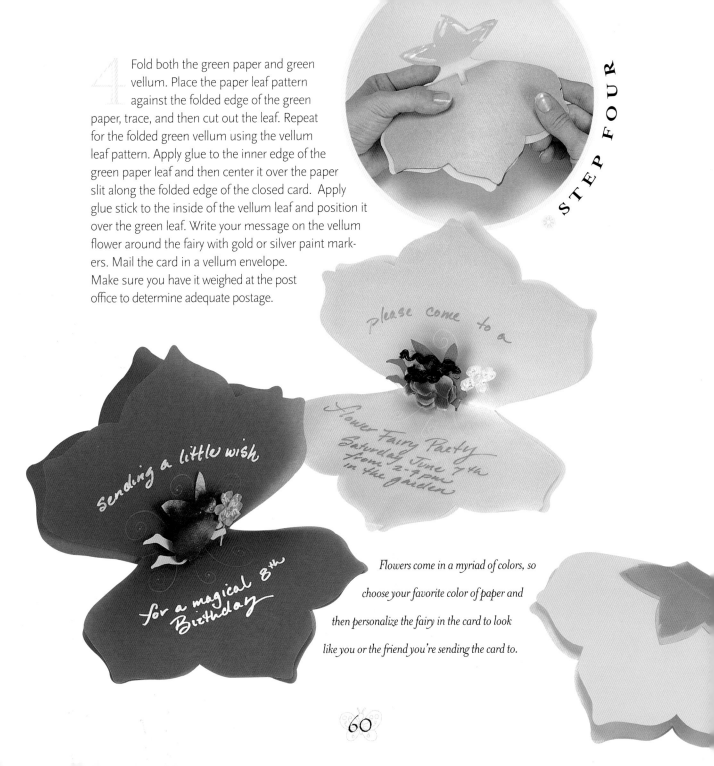

Fold both the green paper and green vellum. Place the paper leaf pattern against the folded edge of the green paper, trace, and then cut out the leaf. Repeat for the folded green vellum using the vellum leaf pattern. Apply glue to the inner edge of the green paper leaf and then center it over the paper slit along the folded edge of the closed card. Apply glue stick to the inside of the vellum leaf and position it over the green leaf. Write your message on the vellum flower around the fairy with gold or silver paint markers. Mail the card in a vellum envelope. Make sure you have it weighed at the post office to determine adequate postage.

sending a little wish

for a magical 8th Birthday

please come to a

Flower Fairy Party Saturday June 7th from 12-4pm in the garden

Flowers come in a myriad of colors, so choose your favorite color of paper and then personalize the fairy in the card to look like you or the friend you're sending the card to.

Petal BRACELETS

Prepare bowls of beads and flower petals and lengths of string at a worktable. Your party guests will have fun sitting together and making something beautiful to take home. They'll be delighted to wear their finished flower bracelets as a party keepsake.

WHAT YOU WILL NEED

- small silk flowers 1½"–2" (4cm–5cm) in diameter
- 1mm clear beading elastic
- iridescent pony beads
- small pearl beads
- scissors

STEP ONE

1 Pull the center out of a flower and slide off both the silk flower petals and the plastic leaf ring. Save both plastic parts and petals and discard the leaves and stems. Continue pulling apart flowers until you have a small bowl for petals and plastic parts for each party guest.

STEP TWO

2 Cut the elastic into 8"–9" (20cm–23cm) lengths. Knot one end of each piece of elastic and start threading flower pieces and beads onto the other end of the elastic. String one flower at a time, starting with a plastic leaf ring followed by a silk flower, pony bead, plastic flower center and then end with a pearl. Bring the ends of the finished bracelet together and tie them in a knot.

flower PLATES

Set your party table abloom with these pretty plates. Trim the edges of paper plates and stack them together to make each flower setting. The finished plates are also great to fill with cookies or candy to deliver to a friend or neighbor.

WHAT YOU WILL NEED

- 10½" (27cm) light green paper plate
- 9" (23cm) lavender or pink paper plate
- 7" (18cm) light yellow paper plate
- pencil
- scissors

NOTE: The paper plates listed above are needed for each individual place setting.

STEP ONE

1 The first plate you make with any of the three cuts will serve as a pattern for the rest of the plates of the same kind. Turn over the large green plate and measure 2½" (6cm) sections around the inner edge of the plate rim for the leaf plate. Repeat for the two smaller plates, measuring 1¼" (3.2cm) sections around the lavender (or pink) plate and 1" (3cm) sections around the small yellow plate.

2 Use a pencil to draw a pointed leaf in each section of the inverted green plate. Make sure the leaf point touches the outside edge of the plate rim. Draw a rounded petal in each section of the lavender plate, again making sure the edge of the rounded petal touches the outside edge of the plate rim. Finally draw a pointed triangle in each section of the yellow plate. Following the pencil lines, cut out the shape of each plate

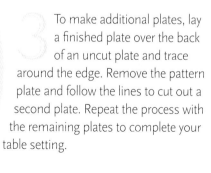

STEP TWO

STEP THREE

3 To make additional plates, lay a finished plate over the back of an uncut plate and trace around the edge. Remove the pattern plate and follow the lines to cut out a second plate. Repeat the process with the remaining plates to complete your table setting.

Blooming
TABLEWARE

Each set of tableware is disguised as a bouquet of blooming flowers. Nestled inside the flower is a sweet bumblebee that is guaranteed not to sting your guests. Arrange the finished bouquets in a basket for a blooming centerpiece or place them around the table at each flowered plate.

WHAT YOU WILL NEED

- pink and lavender disposable plastic tablecloths
- clear or yellow lollipops (remove wrapper and cover with clear cellophane)
- 10mm yellow pom-poms
- small plastic movable eyes
- yellow plastic tableware
- 13" x 13" (33cm x 33cm) 2-ply light green luncheon napkins
- 1/8" (3mm) wide green ribbon
- 22-gauge green floral wire
- 32-gauge white floral wire
- scissors
- wire cutters
- hot glue gun

64

1 Cut 4" (10cm) squares out of both colors of tablecloths. Stack two light pink squares over two lavender squares. Fold the stack in half and then in half again so that you have a folded square that is a quarter of the size of the original. Then fold the square on the diagonal to make a triangle. Cut two half-petal shapes through all the folded layers along the open end of the folded plastic. This can be tricky, as the plastic tends to slip. If you're having trouble, fold and cut only two plastic squares at a time.

2 Discard the cut edges and unfold the cut flowers. Refold them once in half and cut a small slit along the center fold.

3 Cut a 9" (23cm) length of green floral wire for the bee's stripes. Spiral one end of the wire and place the spiral on the backside of a lollipop. Wrap the remaining wire from top to bottom around the lollipop. If necessary, wrap the wire in a loop around the gathered cellophane at the top of the lollipop to help hold it in place. Spiral the wire end at the front of the lollipop and cut off the remaining wire end.

Hot glue a yellow pom-pom head over the wire end, and hot glue two movable eyes onto the head.

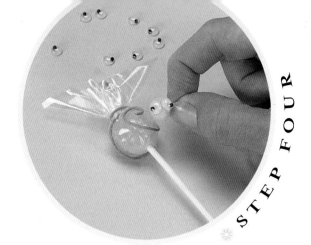

Cut a 2" (5cm) length of white wire for the bee's antennae. Position the center of the wire under the pom-pom, wrap the sides up around the head and twist them together at the top. Bend each wire end into a spiral.

Stack one set of tableware together and position the finished lollipop bee on top. Thread the bottom of the tableware and lollipop down through the center slit of the precut flowers. Slide the flowers up the tableware handles and hold them in place with one hand. With your other hand, fold a napkin in half diagonally, trapping the tableware handles in the center. Fold both sides of the napkin into the center and wrap and tie the folded napkin in place with a 2' (61cm) length of green ribbon.

Butterfly STRAWS

Dress up an ordinary straw with a shimmering butterfly. These fanciful straws will even make an everyday glass of milk fun.

WHAT YOU WILL NEED

- plastic Shimmer Sheetz
- straws
- 32-gauge white floral wire
- pony beads
- pencil
- scissors
- pattern (page 91)

pattern (page 91)

STEP ONE

1 Trace the butterfly pattern onto a Shimmer Sheetz and cut it out. Gently bend the butterfly in half and make two small slits along the center fold. Unfold the butterfly and thread the top of a straw through both slits.

STEP TWO

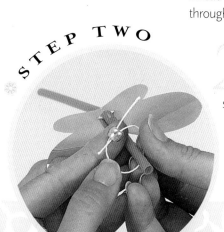

2 Cut a 4" (10cm) length of floral wire and place the center of the wire under the straw. Bring the wire ends up around the sides of the straw. Thread each wire end through a pony bead "head" placed on top of the straw.

3 Use your fingertips to spiral the wire ends into antennae.

STEP THREE

flower FLUTES

Do you think fairies sip juice nectar
from flowers like a hummingbird? These
tall flowering flutes become the focal point
of the party table and are perfect for
lifting together in fairy party toasts.

WHAT YOU WILL NEED

- ❀ pink or purple craft foam sheets
- ❀ acrylic stemware
- ❀ plastic berry beads
- ❀ pearl bead
- ❀ 22-gauge light green floral wire
- ❀ pencil
- ❀ scissors
- ❀ ⅛" (3mm) paper punch
- ❀ pattern (page 91)

TIP

To wash the glasses, you can carefully wipe out the glass cup and try to keep the floral wire dry. If you want to submerge the entire glass in soapy water you'll need to straighten the wire end, remove the beads and slip the wire back out of the foam flower. After the glass has dried, you can replace the shaped floral wire, craft foam flower and beads.

1 Trace the flower pattern on the craft foam sheet and cut out your flower. Depending on the width of your acrylic glass stem, you may need to adjust the size of the flower center. Punch a small hole along the petal edge on either side of the center opening.

2 Spiral one end of a 15" (38cm) length of floral wire and position the spiral at the base of the glass stem. Spiral the wire up the length of the glass stem.

3 Wrap the craft foam flower around the top of the glass stem. Thread the wire through the holes in the flower petals.

4 Thread both a berry and pearl bead onto the wire and spiral the wire end.

69

AUTUMN'S GIFTS

"A hole in one," Daisy called to Lily from her lookout over Chipper's doorway. The chipmunk clicked his approval. Violet bent to take the next walnut from the pile. She lined herself in front of the doorway and gently tossed the ball over the bumpy ground. "Another hole in one," called Daisy. This time the cheers were directed to Violet, who took a shy bow.

The weather had cooled in the garden, and the fairies spent their days helping their friends prepare for the cold winter months ahead. There was a stirring in the grass, and the gathering turned to see Nana Rose appear. "Nana, how are you?" asked Daisy as she flew down from her perch. "Very well, thank you, Daisy," she replied as she tightened her rose petal shawl around her shoulders. Violet bent down to stroke Spot, Nana's faithful companion. The ladybug brushed up against her knee in gratitude. "Chipper, if you could spare the girls, I would like them to help me collect the last petals of the season," Nana asked. "Not a problem, not a problem," clicked Chipper in reply as he set to pushing one walnut at a time with his little nose.

The girls understood the importance of Nana's request. They quickly picked up their purses and wands and flew over to the flower gardens. They circled in and out of the flowers, collecting every last petal. Then they tapped each flower head with their wands. The seeds swirled in the air and landed in the garden soil, where they nestled themselves down for the winter. The smell of warm apple cider guided them to Nana's nook, where they unloaded their purses and warmed their fingers around steaming acorn mugs. Nana shared her most favorite stories of the summer while the four of them tied the petals into pillows. As each sachet was finished, Bumble arrived to deliver it to a fairy in the garden. The petal pillows marked the end of the summer. The fairies lay them under their heads for sweet summer dreams all winter long. As the fairies leaned back in their chairs, weary from their work, Nana reached deep in her pocket and pulled out three sparkling flower necklaces and bracelets for her special helpers. "Oh, Nana, they're beautiful, thank you!" they exclaimed as they encircled her with a hug. Spot squeezed in and brushed against their legs in agreement.

fairy GIFTS

CREATE FLOWER SACHETS AND PRESERVE THE
MAGIC AND FRAGRANCE OF SUMMER FOR YOUR
FRIENDS AND FAMILY. YOU CAN ALSO MAKE
THE VERY SAME GLASS FLOWER BEAD
NECKLACES NANA ROSE PRESENTS IN
THANKS TO DAISY, LILY AND VIOLET. THE
GIFT CHAPTER ALSO FEATURES SPINNING
NOTE CARDS, FAIRY BOOKMARKS AND
FLOWERED PURSES. EACH PRESENT CELEBRATES
SUMMER'S WARMTH AND IS SURE TO BRIGHTEN
EVEN A DREARY WINTER'S DAY.

petal PURSE

This shimmering bag takes minutes to make but will be treasured for years. It can be used to store jewelry and hair accessories and even carry small fairy dolls.

WHAT YOU WILL NEED

- ⅟₄ yard (23cm) of pearlescent sheer fabric (will make several bags)
- bouquet of small bridal flowers
- ⅜" (1cm) wide ribbon with beaded fringe
- ⅛" (3mm) wide ribbon
- scissors
- sewing machine and matching thread
- hot glue gun
- foil or waxed paper (optional)

1 Cut a 16" x 11" (41cm x 28cm) rectangle of pearlescent sheer fabric. Align one side of the 16" (41cm) length along the finished selvage edge of the fabric because it will become the top edge of the finished purse. Fold the fabric in half, right sides together, to make an 8" x 11" (20cm x 28cm) bag. Machine stitch, using a ¼" seam allowance, the cut fabric edges together along one side and the bottom of the purse. Leave the top of the bag open and the folded side unstitched. Turn the purse right side out.

2 Cut the stems off the bridal flowers. Apply a very small amount of glue to the underside of each flower and position them all over the outside of the purse. If you're concerned about the glue leaking through to the other side of the bag, place a piece of foil or waxed paper inside the purse and remove it after the glue has dried. Work until the front and back of the bag shimmers with small flowers.

3 Hot glue a length of beaded fringe over the bottom seam of the purse. To help prevent the ribbon from fraying, turn and glue each ribbon edge under itself to make a finished edge. Close the top of the purse by wrapping a length of ribbon around the fabric and tying the ends into a bow.

flower
JEWELRY

Beautiful yet inexpensive glass beads
are combined with small seed beads to
make these keepsake jewelry pieces.
Learn two simple jewelry techniques that
will make these gifts deceptively easy
to make and durable to wear.
The optional addition of a
fairy charm, which attaches to
the clasp, makes the necklace as beautiful
from the back as it is from the front.

WHAT YOU WILL NEED

- 1" (3cm) and 1½" (4cm) silver head pins
- glass beads (I used Blue Moon beads sold in mixed bags sorted by color.)
- strand of leaf beads (I used Blue Moon beads.)
- small seed beads in green, ivory or ochre (to match the glass beads)
- tiger tail cord (nylon-coated wire that is both smooth and strong)
- silver crimp beads, two per necklace or bracelet
- silver fairy charm (If you can't locate a fairy charm, you can use the jump ring that comes packaged with the spring ring clasp.)
- silver spring ring clasp
- small pliers
- wire cutters

1 Each hanging flower stem is threaded onto a separate head pin. The smaller stems are made with 1" (3cm) pins and the longer stems are made with 1½" (4cm) pins. Beginning with a 1" (3cm) head pin, thread on a round flower center, followed by three flower-shaped beads, a green leaf, and end with four green seed beads.

STEP TWO

2 Use pliers to bend the end of the head pin over into a loop. Repeat the process to make a total of three or five flower stems. Add more flower beads and green beads to fill the 1½" (4cm) long head pins.

STEP THREE

3 Cut a 14" (36cm) length of tiger tail; thread one end of the tiger tail through a crimp bead, and then thread it through a hole in one side of the fairy charm (or jump ring if you're not using the fairy charm). Bring the tiger tail end back through the crimp bead. Holding the end just below the crimp bead, pull gently on the other end of the tiger tail to tighten the loop. Place the pliers over the crimp bead and squeeze it flat.

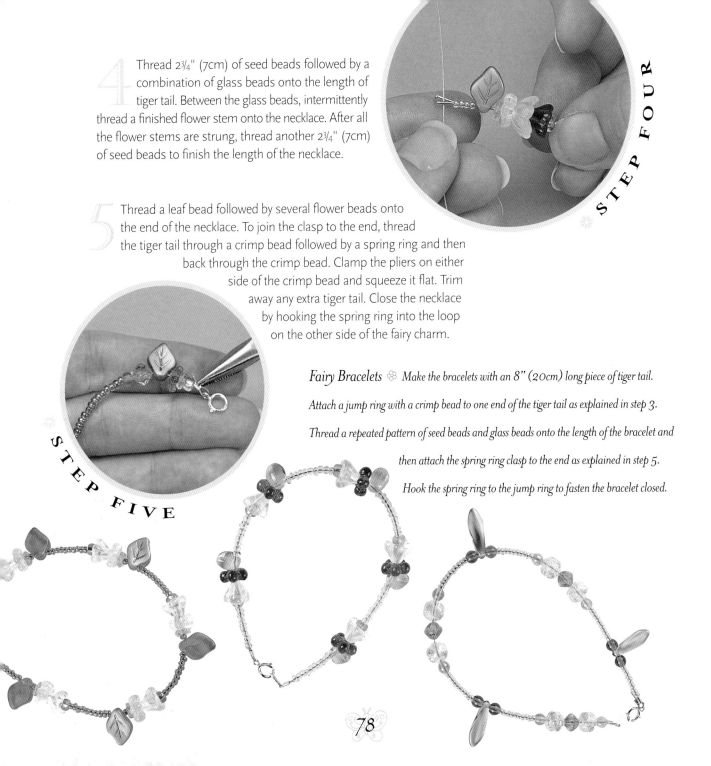

4 Thread 2¾" (7cm) of seed beads followed by a combination of glass beads onto the length of tiger tail. Between the glass beads, intermittently thread a finished flower stem onto the necklace. After all the flower stems are strung, thread another 2¾" (7cm) of seed beads to finish the length of the necklace.

STEP FOUR

5 Thread a leaf bead followed by several flower beads onto the end of the necklace. To join the clasp to the end, thread the tiger tail through a crimp bead followed by a spring ring and then back through the crimp bead. Clamp the pliers on either side of the crimp bead and squeeze it flat. Trim away any extra tiger tail. Close the necklace by hooking the spring ring into the loop on the other side of the fairy charm.

STEP FIVE

Fairy Bracelets ❀ *Make the bracelets with an 8" (20cm) long piece of tiger tail.*

Attach a jump ring with a crimp bead to one end of the tiger tail as explained in step 3.

Thread a repeated pattern of seed beads and glass beads onto the length of the bracelet and then attach the spring ring clasp to the end as explained in step 5.

Hook the spring ring to the jump ring to fasten the bracelet closed.

78

flower SACHETS

Even the youngest children can make this simple sachet with minimal assistance. Match the flowers on top with the scented pellets inside and give as a gift to a special friend.

WHAT YOU WILL NEED

- ⅓ yard (30cm) of 44" (112cm) wide pearlescent sheer crinkle fabric in peach, pink or blue
- fiberfill
- scented pellets
- rubber band
- 20" (51cm) satin cording (one per sachet)
- silk flowers
- scissors
- spoon
- wire cutters
- hot glue gun

1 Cut a 12" (30cm) square of fabric and lay it flat on your work surface. Place a generous handful of fiberfill in the center of the fabric. Pour a couple of spoonfuls of scented pellets over the fiberfill.

STEP ONE

2 Pull the fabric edges up and over the fiberfill and pellets. Wrap a rubber band around the gathered fabric. Tie the center of the cording around the rubber band. Cut the edges off the gathered fabric to leave a flat surface above the tied cord.

STEP TWO

3 After removing a set of leaves and the stem, apply hot glue to the underside of the flower, gluing it over the trimmed fabric. Apply glue to the end of the leaves and tuck them between the flower and fabric.

STEP THREE

79

fairy BOOKMARKS

These bookmarks add a touch of magic to every book you're reading. The ribbon part of the bookmark slides between the pages, the flower hangs over the top of the book, and the fairy spins below. Children who love to color will enjoy making this gift. They'll also be fascinated to watch shrink-art plastic magically shrink in the oven.

WHAT YOU WILL NEED

✿ shrink-art plastic sheets (I used almond-colored sheets.)

✿ fine-tipped paint markers in pastel colors, skin tones and black (Do not substitute a black permanent marker; it will bleed into the paint marker during shrinking.)

✿ 15" (38cm) of ¼" (6mm) wide light green ribbon

✿ small flower (sold in miniature bouquets in the bridal section in craft stores)

✿ clear tape

✿ scissors

✿ paper punch

✿ fairy pattern (page 93)

STEP ONE

1 Place the shrink-art plastic sheet over the pattern (see page 93 for fairy pattern). It's a good idea to tape the pattern to your work surface and then tape the shrink-art plastic sheet over the pattern. This will keep the two from slipping while you work.

STEP TWO

2 Start coloring in between the lines of the image with the lightest color first. (Shake the markers and get the ink flowing on a piece of scrap paper before working on the shrink-art sheet.) After you've colored in the entire image, trace over the black pattern lines with a black paint marker. You can fit up to three fairies on a sheet (see page 92 for color variations).

STEP THREE

3 Carefully cut out each fairy along the outside of the black outlined edge. Shrink-art plastic will tear if you try to bend it while cutting. It's a good idea to roughly cut out each fairy to separate them first and then make finer cuts around each one. Punch a hole through the flower in the fairy's hair and shrink the finished fairy in the oven according to the package instructions.

CAUTION

Supervise your children when using an oven.

4 After the piece has cooled, thread one end of the green ribbon through the hole in the fairy's hair and knot the ribbon end back onto itself. Separate a single flower from the bouquet and tie the other end of the ribbon around the flower stem. Spiral the wire stem end around your finger as a final touch.

81

STEP FOUR

spinning NOTES

A simple trick makes this seemingly flat card open into a spinning butterfly or flower. Be on the lookout for interesting stickers to place in the flower centers. Send a single card to a friend or make an entire set of cards to give as a gift.

WHAT YOU WILL NEED

- 5½" (14cm) square note cards
- yellow, light orange and dark orange tissue paper
- clear elastic (I used Stretch Magic, sold with jewelry-making supplies. You can also use monofilament [fishing line].)
- butterfly stickers (You need two identical stickers for each card.)
- glue stick
- clear tape
- drinking glass, approximately 2¾" (7cm) diameter circle at the base
- pencil
- scissors
- flower pattern (page 93)

1 Place the glass in the center of the note card. Trace around the base of the glass with a pencil to make a circle. Set the glass aside and open the card. Carefully puncture the center of the circle with the scissors point, and cut around the pencil lines to remove the center circle.

2 Place the folded note card over a sheet of yellow tissue paper and trace around all four sides of the card with a pencil. Follow the pencil lines to cut out a tissue-paper square. Spread glue over the back of the square and glue it to the inside of the card where it will show through the opening.

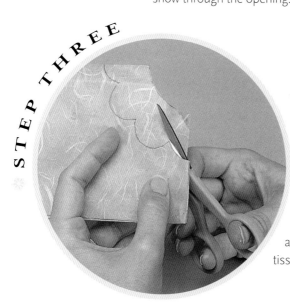

3 Make the flower that encircles the opening on the cover of the card with both light and dark orange tissue-paper sheets. Working with one sheet at a time, fold it in half and then in half again. Position the pattern over the folded tissue-paper point and trace around the pattern with a pencil. Cut along the traced lines through all the folded layers. Adjust the size of the first cut, which will make the hole in the flower, if the opening on the center of your note card is smaller that 2¾" (7cm). Carefully unfold the cut tissue paper into a complete flower. Repeat the process with the second tissue-paper sheet.

4. Glue the back of the dark orange flower around the opening on the front of the card. Glue the back of the light orange flower over the dark orange flower.

5. Open the card. Working on the back side of the cover, lay a 5" (13cm) length of elastic or monofilament down the center of the cut opening. Tape both the top and bottom of the elastic to the card. Place one sticker on the center of the elastic, aligning the center of the butterfly's body with the elastic. Close the card and position the second sticker directly over the first sticker, trapping the elastic between the layers.

Use any combination of two paper colors to make additional cards. The simple color scheme will help show off the sticker. If you're using patterned scrapbook paper, try to find one that is only two shades of the same color.

Spinning Flower Cards ❀ Use a 3" (8cm) square self-stick note as a pattern and place it in the center of the note card. Cut along the lines to make a square opening in the front of the card. Open the card and position a 5" (13cm) length of elastic down the center of the opening. Tape both the top and bottom of the elastic to the card. Make the spinning flower by folding one sheet of tissue paper in half and then in half again. Place the flower pattern over the folded point of the tissue paper and trace around the pattern. Follow the traced lines to cut out the flower. Repeat the process to cut out a second flower. Apply glue to the back of the flower and center it over the taped elastic. Close the card and position the second flower over the first. Punch out two flower centers with a circle hole punch or use a small coin as a pattern to cut two circles.

Glue the circles on either side of the spinning flower. Decorate the envelopes using leftover paper scraps to make a label and then apply a matching sticker to one corner of the label.

patterns: **fairy toys**

Enlarge all templates on pages 86 and 87 by 135%.

Dress-up Fairy Dolls, *page 30*

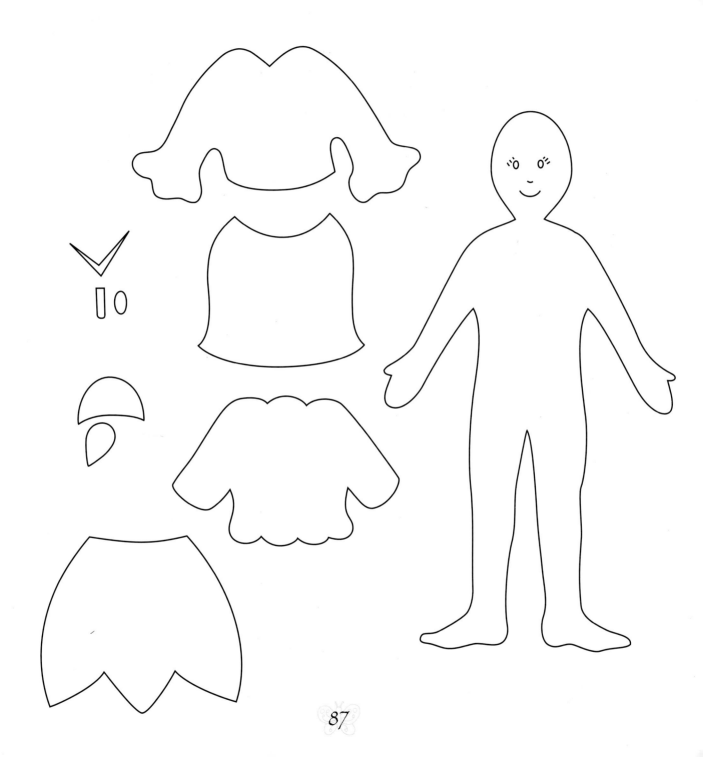

patterns: **fairy costumes**

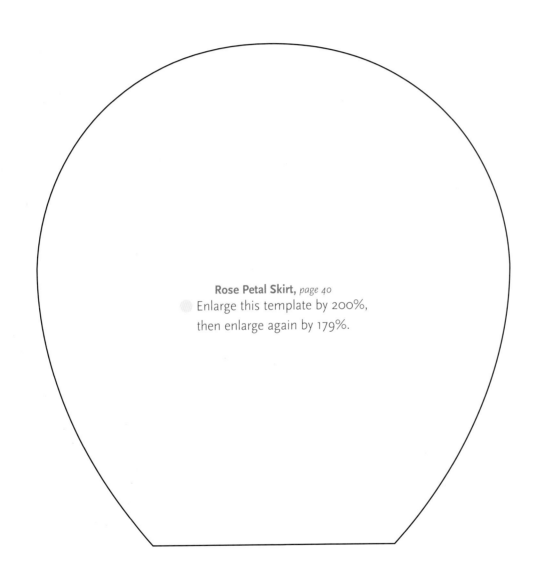

Rose Petal Skirt, *page 40*

Enlarge this template by 200%,
then enlarge again by 179%.

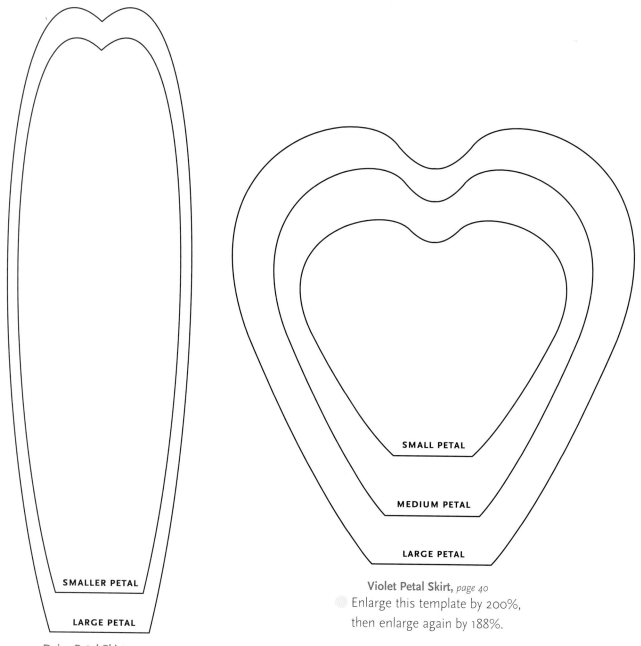

SMALLER PETAL

LARGE PETAL

SMALL PETAL

MEDIUM PETAL

LARGE PETAL

Daisy Petal Skirt, *page 40*
Enlarge this template by 200%,
then enlarge again by 147%.

Violet Petal Skirt, *page 40*
Enlarge this template by 200%,
then enlarge again by 188%.

patterns: **fairy party**

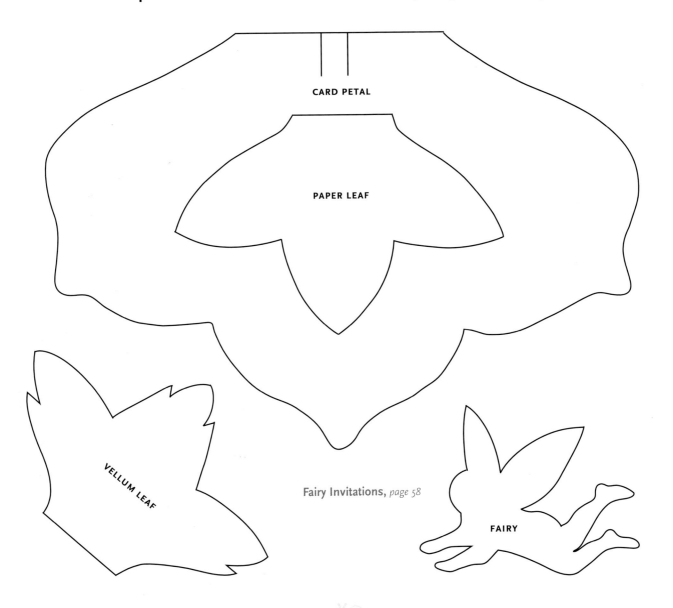

CARD PETAL

PAPER LEAF

VELLUM LEAF

Fairy Invitations, *page 58*

FAIRY

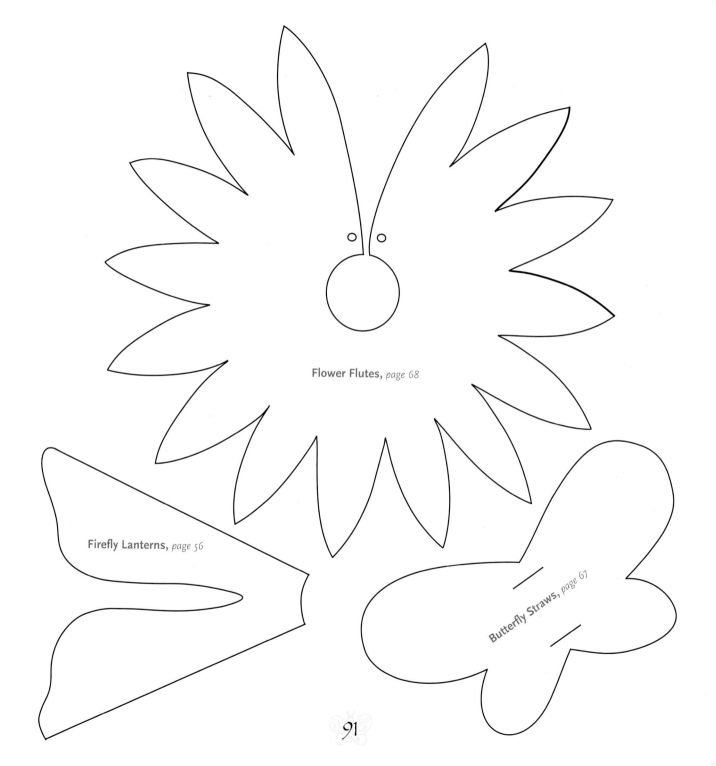

Flower Flutes, *page 68*

Firefly Lanterns, *page 56*

Butterfly Straws, *page 67*

91

patterns: **fairy gifts**

Color Variations for Fairy Bookmarks, *page 80*

SPINNING FLOWER, *page 85*

VARIATION FLOWER, *page 84*

FLOWER

Spinning Notes, *page 82*

Fairy Bookmarks, *page 80*

❀ resources

SHOPPING GUIDE

❀ General craft supplies
available at any arts and crafts stores

❀ Glitter spray, white tights (Fairy Wings); headband (Daisy Headband); acrylic stemware (Flower Flutes); photo album (Dress-up Fairy Dolls); scented pellets (Flower Sachets)
available at any discount store, such as Target (www.target.com)

❀ Mermaid Pearls, pearlescent sheers, shiny tulle fabrics (Petal Skirts)
available at most fabric stores and some arts and crafts stores, such as Jo-Ann (www.joann.com) *and Hobby Lobby* (www.hobbylobby.com)

❀ Paper plates, napkins, tablecloths and tableware (Fairy Party)
available at most paper or party supply stores, such as The Paper Warehouse (www.paperwarehouse.com)

❀ String of lanterns (Firefly Lanterns)
available at most home decor chains, such as Pier 1 (www.pier1.com)

RESOURCE GUIDE

Elizabeth Ward and Co., Inc.
4218 Howard Avenue
Kensington, MD 20895
(800) 377-6715
www.bluemoonbeads.com
❀ Blue Moon beads

FloraCraft Corp.
One Longfellow Place
P.O. Box 400
Ludington, MI 49431
(231) 843-3401
www.floracraft.com
❀ floral foam shapes

Krylon
101 Prospect Ave. NW
Cleveland, OH 44115
(800) 457-9566
www.krylon.com
❀ glitter spray

Polyform Products Co.
1901 Estes Ave.
Elk Grove Village IL 60007
(847) 427-0020
www.sculpey.com
❀ Sculpey III Polymer clay

Signature Crafts
P.O. Box 427
Wycoff, NJ 07481
(800) 865-7238
www.beaconcreates.com
❀ Kid's Choice, Hold the Foam, CraftFoam, Fabri-Tac and Gem-Tac glues

Sulyn Industries Inc.
11927 W. Sample Rd.
Coral Springs, FL 33065
(800) 257-8596
www.sulyn.com
❀ Shimmer Sheetz

index

Get creative with these other fun books for kids!

Painting on Rocks for Kids Hey kids! You can create amazing creatures, incredible toys and wild gifts for your friends and family. All it takes is some paint, a few rocks and your imagination! Easy-to-follow pictures and instructions show you how to turn stones into something cool—racecars, bugs, lizards, teddy bears and more. ISBN 1-58180-255-2, paperback, 64 pages, #32085-K

Nature Crafts You can make incredible crafts using materials found just outside your window! Learn how to create pressed flower bookmarks, clay tiles, leaf prints, pebble mosaics, nature mobiles and souvenir pillows. You can use collected leaves, rocks, feathers and other natural treasures. ISBN 1-58180-292-7, paperback, 64 pages, #32169-K

Paper Creations Oh, the things you can create with paper! Learn how to make paper stars, party streamers, lanterns, hanging baskets, paper beads, handmade books, decoupage and more. These crafts are perfect for parties, rainy days and gift giving, plus they're easy to do and fun to make. ISBN 1-58180-290-0, paperback, 64 pages, #32167-K

Clay Characters for Kids Mold polymer clay into a fantasy world right out of your imagination! Maureen Carlson shows you how to sculpt 10 easy shapes that can be used to create dozens of different creatures and characters, including dragons, goblins, fairies, ghosts, pigs, dogs, horses, bunnies and more. ISBN 1-58180-286-2, paperback, 80 pages, #32161-K

These and other fun North Light Books for Kids are available from your local art & craft retailer, bookstore, online supplier or by calling 1-800-448-0915.